MARY JONES AND HER BIBLE

MARY JONES
AND HER
BIBLE

By M.E.R.

GOSPEL STANDARD TRUST PUBLICATIONS

1996

12(b) Roundwood Lane,

Harpenden, Herts. AL5 3DD, England

ISBN 0 903556 69 3

© Gospel Standard Trust Publications 1987
1st Reprint 1985
2nd Reprint 1987
3rd Reprint 1989
4th Reprint 1991
5th Reprint 1994
6th Reprint 1996

Cover photo: Tal-y-llyn, Wales

*Printed in Great Britain
by Chandlers Printers Ltd.,
Bexhill-on-Sea, East Sussex*

PREFACE.

IT was in the spring of 1800 that an unknown Welsh girl set out barefooted from her home in Llanfihangel to walk to Bala— a distance of twenty-five miles. The purpose of her journey was to buy a Bible for which she had been saving up for several years. Thomas Charles of Bala was so impressed by Mary Jones's love for the Word of God, and so grieved because of the scarcity of Bibles in Welsh, that he had no rest till a society for the printing of Bibles was formed. How thankful we should be that today the Word of God is so readily available translated into our native tongue!

The original account of Mary Jones was published by the British and Foreign Bible Society in 1882, since when her name has been know throughout the world. It is this original account, long out of print, which is now re-published (with the kind agreement of the Bible Society). The book is reproduced from the 1896 edition and so appears with all the typical Victorian pictures and engravings. We are indebted to friends for the photograph on the cover and the detailed information at the end concerning the "Mary Jones country."

Who the authoress, M. E. R., was we do not know but certainly she was a lucid and interesting writer.

Gospel Standard Trust Publications are re-publishing *Mary Jones and Her Bible* as a witness to the power of God's Word in a young girl's heart, and with the prayerful desire that it may be blessed to our children today. However, the phraseology is different from ours and we cannot agree with every expression—especially the legal tone in places and the occasional reference to luck, chance and fortune (pages 22, 55, 61, 72, 92, 105, 120). As the book is copied by lithography from the last century edition, it was not possible to make amendments.

May the Lord again make known the power of His Word by the Holy Spirit throughout the earth, not least in once highly favoured Wales.

March 1987   *Gospel Standard Trust Publications*

CONTENTS.

A GLIMPSE OF CADER IDRIS.

CHAPTER I.

AT THE FOOT OF THE MOUNTAIN.

O Shepherd of all the flock of God,
Watch over Thy lambs and feed them ;
For Thou alone, through the rugged paths,
In the way of life canst lead them.

It would be hard to find a lovelier, more
picturesque spot than the valley on the

south-west side of Cader Idris, where nestles the little village of Llanfihangel-y-Pennant. Above it towers the majestic mountain with its dark crags, its rocky precipices, and its steep ascents ; while stretching away in the distance to the westward, lie the bold shore and glistening waters of Cardigan Bay, where the white breakers come rolling in and dash into foam, only to gather afresh, and return undaunted to the charge.

The mountain, and the outline of the bay, and the wonderful picturesqueness of the valley, are still much as they were a hundred years ago. Still the eye of the traveller gazes in wonder at their wild beauty, as other eyes of other travellers did in times gone by. But while Nature's great landmarks remain, or undergo a change so gradual as to be almost imperceptible, man, the tenant of God's earth, is born, lives his brief life, and passes away, leaving only too often hardly even a memory behind him.

And now as, in thought, we stand upon the lower slopes of Cader Idris, and look across the little village of Llanfihangel, we find ourselves wondering what kind of people have occupied those rude grey cottages for the last century ; what were their simple histories, what their habits, their toils and struggles, sorrows and pleasures.

To those then who share our interest in the place and neighbourhood, and in events connected with them, we would tell the simple tale which gives Llanfihangel a place among the justly celebrated and honoured spots of our beloved country ; since from its soil sprang a shoot which, growing apace, soon spread forth great branches throughout the earth, becoming indeed a tree of life, whose leaves are for the healing of the nations.

In the year 1792, nearly a hundred years ago, the night shadows had fallen around the little village of Llanfihangel. The season was late autumn, and a cold wind was moaning and sighing among the trees, stripping them of their changed garments, lately so green and gay, whirling them round in eddies and laying them in shivering heaps along the narrow valley

Wan and watery, the moon, encompassed by peaked masses of cloud that looked like another ghostly Cader Idris in the sky, had risen, and now cast a faint light across a line of jutting crags, bringing into relief their sharp ragged edges against the dark background of rolling vapour.

In pleasant contrast to the night with its threatening gloom, a warm light shone through the windows of one of the cottages that formed the village. The light was caused by the blaze of a fire of dried driftwood on the stone hearth, while in a rude wooden stand a rushlight burned, throwing its somewhat uncertain brightness upon a loom where sat a weaver at work. A bench, two or three stools, a rude cupboard, and a kitchen-table—these, with the loom, were all the furniture.

A WELSH COTTAGE.

Standing in the centre of the room was a middle-aged woman, dressed in a cloak and the tall conical Welsh hat worn by many of the peasants to this day.

"I am sorry you cannot go, Jacob," said she. "You'll be missed at the meeting. But the same Lord Almighty who gives us the meetings for the good of our souls, sent you that wheezing of the chest, for the trying of your body and spirit, and we must needs have patience till He sees fit to take it away again."

"Yes, wife, and I'm thankful that I needn't sit idle, but can still ply my trade," replied Jacob Jones. "There's many a deal worse off. But what are you waiting for, Molly? You'll be late for the exercises; it must be gone six o'clock."

"I'm waiting for that child, and she's gone for the lantern," responded Mary Jones, whom her husband generally called Molly, to distinguish her from their daughter who was also Mary.

Jacob smiled. " The lantern ! Yes," said he ; " you'll need it this dark night. 'Twas a good thought of yours, wife, to let Mary take it regular as you do, for the child wouldn't be allowed to attend those meetings otherwise. And she does seem so eager after everything of the kind."

" Yes, she knows already pretty nearly all that you and I can teach her of the Bible, as we learnt it, don't she, Jacob ? She's only eight now, but I remember when she was but a wee child she would sit on your knee for hours on a Sunday, and hear tell of Abraham and Joseph, and David and Daniel. There never was a girl like our Mary for Bible stories, or any stories, for the matter of that, bless her ! But here she is ! You've been a long time getting that lantern, child, and we must hurry or we shall be late."

Little Mary raised a pair of bright dark eyes to her mother's face.

"Yes, mother," she replied, " I was long because I ran to borrow neighbour Williams's lantern. The latch of ours won't hold, and there's such a wind to-night, that I knew we should have the light blown out."

" There's a moon," said Mrs. Jones, " and I could have done without a lantern."

" Yes, but then you know, mother, I should have had to stay at home," responded Mary, " and I do so love to go."

" You needn't tell me that, child," laughed Molly. " Then come along, Mary; good-bye, Jacob."

" Good-bye, father dear! I wish you could come too!" cried Mary, running back to give Jacob a last kiss.

" Go your way, child, and mind you remember all you can to tell old father when you come home."

Then the cottage door opened. and Mary and her mother sallied out into the cold windy night.

The moon had disappeared now behind a thick dark cloud, and little Mary's borrowed lantern was very acceptable. Carefully she held it, so that the light fell upon the way they had to traverse, a way which would have been difficult if not dangerous, without its friendly aid.

" Thy Word is a lamp unto my feet, and a light unto my path," said Mrs. Jones, as she took her little daughter's hand in hers.

" Yes, mother, I was just thinking of that," replied the child. " I wish I knew ever so many verses like this one."

" How glad I should be if your father and I could teach you more ; but it's years since we learned, and we've got no Bible, and our memories are not as good as they used to be," sighed the mother.

A walk of some length, and over a rough road, brought them at last to the little meeting-house where the church members belonging to the Methodist body were in the habit of attending.

They were rather late, and the exercises had begun, but kind farmer Evans made room for them on his bench, and found for

Mrs. Jones the place in the psalm-book from which the little company had been singing. Mary was the only child there, but her face was so grave, and her manner so solemn and reverent, that no one looking at her could have felt that she was out of place ; and the church members who met there from time to time, had come to look upon this little girl as one of their number, and welcomed her accordingly.

When the meeting was over, and Mary, having relighted her lantern, was ready to accompany her mother home, farmer Evans put his great broad hand upon the child's shoulder, saying :

" Well, my little maid ! You're rather young for these meetings, but the Lord has need of lambs as well as sheep, and He is well pleased when the lambs learn to hear His voice early, even in their tender years."

Then with a gentle fatherly caress the good old man released the child, and turned away, carrying with him the remembrance of that earnest intelligent face, happy in its intentness, joyful in its solemnity, having in its expression a promise of future excellence and power for good.

"Why haven't we a Bible of our own, mother?" asked Mary as she trotted homeward, lantern in hand.

"Because Bibles are scarce, child, and we're too poor to pay the price of one. A weaver's is an honest trade, Mary, but we don't get rich by it, and we think ourselves happy if we can keep the wolf from the door, and have clothes to cover us. Still, precious as the Word of God would be in our hands, more precious are its teachings and its truths in our hearts. I tell you, my little girl, they who have learned the love of God, have learned the greatest truth that even the Bible can teach them ; and those who are trusting the Saviour for their pardon and peace, and for eternal life at last, can wait patiently for a fuller knowledge of His word and will."

"I suppose you can wait, mother, because

you've waited so long that you're used to it,"
replied the child; "but it's harder for me.
Every time I hear something read out of
the Bible, I long to hear more, and when I
can read it will be harder still."

Mrs. Jones was about to answer, when
she stumbled over a stone, and fell, though
fortunately without hurting herself. Mary's
thoughts were so full of what she had been
saying, that she had become careless in the
management of the lantern, and her mother
not seeing the stone, had struck her foot
against it.

"Ah, child! it's the present duties after
all that we must look after most," said Molly,
as she got slowly up; "and even a fall may
teach us a lesson, Mary. The very Word
of God itself, which is a lamp to our feet,
and a light to our path, can't save us from
many a tumble if we don't use it aright, and
let the light shine on our daily life, helping
us in its smallest duties and cares. Remember
this, my little Mary."

And little Mary did remember this, and her after life proved that she had taken the lesson to heart—a simple lesson, taught by a simple, unlearned handmaid of the Lord, but a lesson which the child treasured up in her very heart of hearts.

Chained Bibles.

CHAPTER II.

THE ONE GREAT NEED.

For this I know, whate'er of earthly good
Fall to the portion of immortal man,
Still unfulfill'd in him is God's great plan,
And Heaven's richest gift misunderstood,
Until the Word of Life—exhaustless store
Of light and truth—be his for evermore.

IN the homes of the poor, where the time of the elder members of the family is precious, they being the bread-winners of the household, the little ones learn to be useful very early. How often we have known girls of six to take the entire charge of a younger brother and sister, while many children of that age run errands, do simple shopping, and make themselves of very real and substantial use.

Such was the case in the family of Jacob Jones. Jacob and Molly were engaged in weaving the woollen cloth, so much of which used to be made in Wales. Thus many of the household duties devolved upon Mary ; and at an age when children of richer parents are amusing themselves with their dolls or picture-books, our little maid was sweeping, and dusting, and scrubbing, and digging and weeding.

It was Mary who fed the few hens, and looked for their eggs, so often laid in queer, wrong places, rather than in the nest.

It was Mary who took care of the hive, and who never feared the bees ; and it was Mary again, who, when more active duties were done, would draw a low stool towards the hearth in winter or outside the cottage door in summer, and try to make or mend her own little simple garments, singing to herself the while in Welsh, a verse or two of the old-fashioned metrical version of the Psalms, or repeating texts which she had picked up and retained in her quick, eager little brain.

In the long, light summer evenings, it was her delight to sit where she could see the majestic form of Cader Idris with its varying lights and shadows, as the sun sank lower and lower in the horizon. And in her childish imagination, this mountain was made to play many a part, as she recalled the stories which her parents had told her, and the chapters she had heard read at chapel.

Now, Cader Idris was the mountain in the land of Moriah whither the patriarch was sent on his painful mission; and Mary would fix her great dark eyes upon the rocky steeps before her, until she fancied she could see the venerable Abraham and his son toiling up towards the appointed place of sacrifice, the lad bearing the wood for the burnt-offering.

More and more vividly the whole scene would grow upon the child's fancy, until the picture seemed to be almost a reality, and she could imagine that she heard the patriarch's voice borne faintly to her ear by the breeze that fanned her cheek—a voice that replied pathetically to his son's question, in the words, " My son, the Lord will provide Himself a lamb for the burnt-offering."

Then the scene would change ; night was drawing near, and Cader Idris assuming softer outlines, was the mountain where the Saviour went to pray.

Leaving the thronging multitude who had been dwelling upon His every word—leaving even His disciples whom He so loved, there was Jesus—alone save for the Eternal Father's presence—praying, and refreshing thus His weary spirit, after the work and trials and sorrows of the day.

" If I'd only lived in those days," sighed little Mary, sometimes, " how I should have loved Him ! and He'd have taught me, perhaps, as He did those two who walked such a long way with Him, without knowing that it was Jesus; only I think *I* should have known Him, just through love."

Nor was it only the mountain with which Mary associated scenes from sacred history or Gospel narration. The long, narrow valley in the upper end of which Llanfihangel was situated, ran down to the sea at no great distance by a place called Towyn. And when the child happened to be near, she would steal a few moments to sit down on the shore, and gaze across the blue-green waters of Cardigan Bay, and dream of the Sea of Galilee, and of the Saviour who walked upon its waters— who stilled their raging with a word, and who even sometimes chose to make His pulpit of a boat, and preach thus to the congregation that stood upon the shore and clustered to the very edge of the water, so that they might not lose a word of the precious things that He spoke. It will be seen, therefore, that upon Mary's mind a deep and lasting impression was made by all that she had heard; and child though she might be in years, there were not wanting in her evidences of an earnest, energetic nature, an intelligent brain, and a warm, loving heart.

It is by the first leaves put forth by the seedling that we discern the nature, and know the name of the plant; and so in childhood, the character and talents can often be detected in the early beauty of their first unfolding and development.

One afternoon, when Jacob and his wife were seated at their looms, and Mary was sewing a patch into an almost worn-out garment of her own, a little tap at the door was followed by the entrance of Mrs. Evans, the good farmer's wife, a kind, motherly, and in some respects superior woman, who was looked up to and beloved by many of the Llanfihangel villagers.

"Good day to you, neighbours!" she said,

cheerily, her comely face all aglow. " Jacob,
how is your chest feeling ?   Bad, I'm afraid,
as I haven't seen you out of late.   Molly,
you're looking   hearty as   usual,   and   my
little   Mary,   too—Toddles,   as   I   used   to
call   you   when   you   were   not   much   more
than   a   baby,   and   running   round   on   your
sturdy   pins   as   fast   as   many   **a**   bigger   child.
Don't   I   remember   you   then !   A   mere
baby   as   I   said,   and   yet   you'd   keep   a   deal
stiller   than   any   mouse   if   your   father   there
would   make   up   a   story   you   could   understand,
more   particular   if   it   was   out   of   the   Bible.
Daniel   and   the   Lions,   or   David   and   the
Giant,   or   Peter   in   the   Prison—these   were   the
favourites   then.   Yes,   and   the   history   of
Joseph   and   his   brethren ;   only   you   used   to
cry   when   the   naughty   brothers   put   Joseph
in   the   pit,   and   went   home   and   told   Jacob
that   wicked   lie   that   almost   broke   the   old
man's   heart."

   " She's   as   fond   of   anything   of   that   sort
now   as   she   was   then,"   said   Jacob   Jones,

pausing in his work ; " or rather she's fonder
than ever, ma'am.   I only wish we were able
to give her a bit of schooling.   It seems
hard, for the child is willing enough, and
it's high time she was learning something.
Why, Mrs. Evans, she can't read yet, and
she's eight years old ! "

Mary looked up, her face flushing, her
eyes filled with tears.

" Oh !   If I only could learn ! " she cried,
eagerly.   " I'm such a big girl, and it's so
dreadful not to know how to read.   If I
could, I would read all the lovely stories
myself, and not trouble any one to tell
them."

" You forget, Mary, we've no Bible," said
Molly Jones, " and we can't afford to buy
one either, so dear and scarce they are."

" Yes," replied Mrs. Evans, " it's a great
want in our country ; my husband was telling
me only the other day that the scarcity of
Welsh Bibles is getting to be spoken of
everywhere.   Even those who can afford to

pay for them get them with difficulty, and only by bespeaking them ; and poor people can't get them at all. But we hope the Society for Christian Knowledge in London may print some more soon ; it won't be before they're wanted."

"But with all this talk, Mrs. Jones," continued the farmer's wife, "I am forgetting my errand in coming here, and that was to ask if you'd any new-laid eggs. I've a large order sent me, and our hens are laying badly, so that I can't make up the number. I've been collecting a few here and there, but I haven't enough yet."

"Mary knows more about the hens and eggs than I do," said Molly, looking at her little daughter, who had not put a stitch into her patch while the talk about Bibles had been going on, and whose cheeks and eyes showed in their deepened colour and light how much interested she had been in what had been said.

But now the child started half guiltily

from her low seat, saying, " I'll get what we have to show you, Mrs. Evans."

Presently she came in with a little basket containing about a dozen eggs. The farmer's wife put them into her bag, then patting Mary's pink cheeks rose to take her leave, after paying for the eggs.

" And remember this, little maid," she said, kindly, when after saying good-bye to Jacob and Molly, she was taking leave of Mary at the door. " Remember this, my dear little girl ; as soon as you know how to read (if by that time you still have no Bible) you shall come to the farm when you like, and read and study ours — that is, if you can manage to get so far."

" It's only two miles, that's nothing ! " said sturdy Mary, with a glance down at her strong little bare feet. " I'd walk further than that for such a pleasure, ma'am." Then she added with a less joyful ring in her voice, " At least I would, if ever I *did* learn to read."

" Never mind, little woman ! The likes of you wasn't made to sit in the dark always," replied Mrs. Evans in her cheery, comfortable tones. " The Lord made the want, and He'll satisfy it ; be very sure of that. Remember, Mary, when the multitude that waited on the Saviour were hungry, the Lord did not send them away empty, though no one saw how they were to be fed ; and He'll take care you get the bread of life too, for all it seems so unlikely now. Good-bye, and God bless you, my child ! " and good Mrs. Evans, with a parting nod to the weaver and his wife, and another to Mary, went out, and got into her little pony-cart, which was waiting for her in the road, under the care of one of the farm-boys.

Mary stood at the door and watched their visitor till she was out of sight. Then, before she closed it, she clasped her small brown hands against her breast, and her thoughts formed themselves into a prayer something like this :

"Dear Lord, who gavest bread to the hungry folk in the old time, and didst teach and bless even the poorest, please let me learn, and not grow up in darkness."

Then she shut the door and came and sat down, resolving in her childish heart that if God heard and answered her prayer, and she learned to read His Word, she would do what she could, all her life long, to help others as she herself had been helped.

How our little Mary kept her resolution will be seen in the remaining chapters of this simple narrative.

Tail-piece from Coverdale's New Test., 1538, *in the Library or the Bible Society.*

LLAN-Y-CIL BAY, BALA LAKE.

CHAPTER III.

COMING TO THE LIGHT.

O thou who out of the darkness
    Reachest thy trembling hand,
Whose ears are open to welcome
    Glad news of a better land ;
Not always shalt thou be groping,
    Night's shadows are well-nigh past :
The heart that for light is yearning
    Attains to that light at last.

TWO years had passed away since Mrs.
Evans's visit, as recorded in the pre-

ceding chapter, and still little Mary's prayer seemed as far as ever from being answered.

With the industry and patience of more mature years the child went about her daily duties, and her mother depended upon her for many things which do not generally form part of a child's occupations. Mary had less time for dreaming now, and though Cader Idris was still the spot with which her imagination associated Bible scenes and pictures, she had little leisure for anything but her everyday duties. She still accompanied her mother to the meetings, and from so continually coming into contact with older people, rather than with children of her own age, the child had grown more and more grave and earnest in face and manner, and would have been called an old-fashioned girl if she had lived in a place where any difference was known between old fashions and new.

It was about this time that Jacob Jones came home one evening from Abergynolwyn

—a village two miles away from Llanfihangel —where he had been disposing of the woollen cloth which he and Molly had been making during the past months.

Jacob had been away the greater part of the day, yet he did not seem tired.   His eye was bright, and his lips wore a smile as he entered the cottage and sat down in his accustomed place in the chimney corner.

Mary, whose observant eye rarely failed to note the least change in her father's face and manner, sprang towards him, and stood before him, regarding his bright face searchingly.

" What is it, father ? " she said, her own dark eyes flashing back the light in his. " Something pleasant has happened, or you wouldn't look like that ! "

" What a sharp little girl it is ! " replied Jacob, fondly, drawing the child nearer and seating her upon his knee.   " What a very sharp little woman to find out that her old dad has something to tell ! "

" And is it something that concerns me,

father ? " asked Mary, stroking Jacob's face caressingly.

" It *is* something that concerns you most of all, my chick, and us through you."

" What can it be ? " murmured Mary, with a quick, impatient little sigh.

" What is it, father ? " asked Mrs. Jones ; " we both want to know."

" Well," replied Jacob, " what would you say, Molly dear, to our little daughter here becoming quite a learned woman, perhaps knowing how to read, and write, and cipher, and all a deal better than her parents ever did before her ? "

" Oh, father ! "

The exclamation came from Mary, who in her excitement had slipped from Jacob's knee, and now stood facing him, breathless with suspense, her hands closely clasped.

Jacob looked at her a moment without speaking ; then he said tenderly :

" Yes, child, there *is* a school to be opened at Abergynolwyn, and a master is chosen already ; and as my little Mary thinks nought of a two miles' walk, she shall go, and learn all she can."

" Oh, father ! "

" Well," rejoined Jacob, now laughing out-right, " how many ' Oh fathers ! ' are we going to have ? But I thought you'd be glad, my girl, and I was not wrong. You are pleased, dear, aren't you ? "

There was a pause ; then Mary's reply came, low spoken, but with such deep content in its tones.

" Pleased, father ? Yes, indeed, for now I shall learn to read the Bible."

Then a thought struck her, and a shadow came across the happy face as she said :

" But, mother, perhaps you won't be able to spare me ? "

"Spare you ? Yes, I will, child, though I can't deny as how it will be difficult for me to do without my little right hand and help. But for your good, my girl, I would do harder things than that."

" Dear, good mother !" cried Mary, putting
an arm about Molly's neck and kissing her.
" But I don't want you to work too hard and
tire yourself. I'll get up an hour or two
earlier, and do all I can before I start for
school." Then as the child sat down again
to her work, her heart, in its joyfulness, sent
up a song of thanksgiving to the Lord who
had heard her prayer, and opened the way
for her to learn, that she might not grow up
in darkness.

Presently Jacob went on :

" I went to see the room where the school
is to be held, and who should come in while
I was there but Mr. Charles of Bala. I'd
often heard of him before, but I'd never
seen him, and I was glad to set eyes on him
for once."

" What may he have looked like, Jacob ? "
asked Molly.

" Well, Molly, I never was a very good one
for drawing a portrait, but I should say he
was between forty and fifty years old, with

THE REV. THOMAS CHARLES, OF BALA.
(*From the painting in the Bible House.*)

a fine big forehead which doesn't look as though it had unfurnished apartments to let behind it, but quite the opposite, as though he had done a sight of thinking, and meant to do a great deal more. Still his face isn't anything so *very* special till he smiles, but when he does it's like sunshine, and goes to your heart, and warms you right through. Now I've seen him, and heard him speak, I can understand how he does so much good. I hear he's going about from place to place opening schools for the poor children, who would grow up ignorant otherwise."

"Like me," murmured Mary, under her breath.

"And who's the master that's to be set over the school at Abergynolwyn?" asked Molly.

"I heard tell that his name is John Ellis," replied Jacob; "a good man, and right for the work, so they say; and I hope it'll prove so."

"And how soon is the school to open, Jacob?" asked his wife.

"In about three weeks, I believe," answered Jacob. "And now, Mary my girl, if you can bring yourself to think of such a thing as supper, after what I've been telling you, suppose you get some ready, for I haven't broke my fast since noon."

The following three weeks passed more slowly for little Mary Jones than any three months she could remember before. Such childishness as there was in her seemed to show itself in impatience; and we must confess that her home duties at this time were not so cheerfully or so punctually performed as usual, owing to the fact that her thoughts were far away, her heart being set on the thing she had longed for so earnestly.

"If *this* is the way it's going to be, Jacob," said Molly to her husband one evening, "I shall wish there had never been a thought of school at Abergynolwyn. The child's so off her head that she goes about like one in a dream; what it'll be when that school begins, I daren't think."

"Don't you fret, wife," replied Jacob smiling. "It'll all come right. Don't you see that her poor little busy brain has been longing to grow, and now that there's a chance of its being fed, she's all agog. But you'll find, when she once gets started, she'll go on all right with her home work as well. She's but ten years old, Molly, after all, and for my own part, I'm not sorry to see there's a bit of the child left in her, even if it shows itself this way, such a little old woman as she's always been!"

But this longest three weeks that Mary ever spent came to an end at last, and Mary began to go to school, thus commencing a new era in her life.

Fairly hungering and thirsting after knowledge, the child found her lessons an unmixed delight. What other children call drudgery was to her only pleasure, and her eagerness was so great that she was almost always at the top of her class ; and in an incredibly short space of time she began to read and write.

The master, who had a quick eye for observing the character and talents of his pupils, soon remarked Mary's peculiarities, and encouraged her in her pursuit of such knowledge as was taught in the school ; and the little girl repaid her master's kindness by the most unwearied diligence and attention.

Nor while the brain was being fed did the heart grow cold, or the practical powers decline. Molly Jones had now no fault to find with Mary's performance of her home duties. The child rose early, and did her work before breakfast ; and after her return from school in the afternoon she again helped her mother, only reserving for herself time enough to prepare her lessons for the next day.

At school she was a general favourite, and never seemed to be regarded with jealousy by her companions, this being due probably to her genial disposition, and the kind way in which she was willing to help others whenever she could.

One morning a little girl was seen to be crying sadly when she reached the school-house, and on being questioned as to what was the matter, she said that on the way there, a big dog had snatched at the little paper bag in which she was bringing her dinner to eat during recess, and had carried it off, and so she should have to go hungry all day.

Some of the scholars laughed at the child for her carelessness, and some called her a coward, for not running after the dog and getting back her dinner ; but Mary stole up to the little one's side, and whispered something in her ear, and dried the wet eyes, and kissed the flushed cheeks, and presently the child was smiling and happy again.

But when dinner-time came, Mary and the little dinnerless maiden sat close together in a corner, and more than half of Mary's provisions found their way to the smaller child's mouth.

The other scholars looked on, feeling

somewhat ashamed, no doubt, that none but Mary Jones had thought of doing so kind and neighbourly an action, at the cost of a little self-denial. But the lesson was not lost upon them, and from that day Mary's influence made itself felt in the school for good.

In her studies she progressed steadily, and this again gave opportunity for the development of the helpful qualities by which, from her earliest childhood, she had been distinguished.

On one occasion, for instance, she was just getting ready to set off on her two miles' journey home, when she spied in a corner of the now deserted schoolroom a little boy with a book open before him, and a smeared slate and blunt pencil by its side. The poor little fellow's tears were falling over his unfinished task, and evidently he was in the last stage of childish despondency. He had dawdled away his time during the school hours, or had not listened when the lesson had been explained, and now school discipline required that he should stay behind when the rest had gone, and attend to the work which he had neglected.

Mary had a headache that day, and was longing to get home ; but the sight of that tearful, sad little face in the corner banished all thought of self, and as the voices of the other children died away in the distance, she crossed the room, and leaned over the small student's shoulder.

" What is it, Robbie dear ? " said she in her old-fashioned way and tender, low-toned voice. " Oh, I see, you've got to do that sum! I mayn't do it for you, you know, because that would be a sort of cheating, but I can tell you how to do it yourself, and I think I can make it plain."

So saying, Mary fetched her little bit of wet rag, and washed the slate, and then got an old knife and sharpened the pencil.

" Now," said she, smiling cheerily, " see, I'll put down the sum as it is in the book ;"

and she wrote on the slate in clear, if not very elegant figures, the sum in question.

Thus encouraged, Robbie gave his mind to his task, and with a little help it was soon done, and Mary with a light heart, which made up for her heavy head, trotted home, very glad that what she was herself learning could be a benefit to others.

Not long after the commencement of the day school, a Sunday school also was opened, and the very first Sunday that children were taught there, behold our little friend as clean and fresh as soap and water could make her, and with bright eyes and eager face, showing the keen interest she felt, and her great desire to learn.

That evening, after service in the little meeting-house, as the farmer's wife, good Mrs. Evans, was just going to get into her pony-cart to drive home, she felt a light touch on her arm, while a sweet voice she knew said, "Please, ma'am, might I speak to you a moment?"

" Surely, my child," replied the good woman, turning her beaming face on little Mary, " what have you got to say to me?"

" Two years ago, please ma'am, you were so kind as to promise that when I'd learned to read I should come to the farm and read your Bible."

" I did, I remember it well," answered Mrs. Evans. "Well, child, do you know how to read ? "

" Yes, ma'am," responded Mary ; " and now I've joined the Sunday school, and shall have Bible lessons to prepare, and if you'd be so kind as to let me come up to the farm one day in the week—perhaps Saturday, when I've a half-holiday—I could never thank you enough."

" There's no need for thanks, little woman, come and welcome ! I shall expect you next Saturday ; and may the Lord make His Word a great blessing to you ! "

Mrs. Evans held Mary's hand one moment with a cordial pressure ; then she got into her cart, and the pony started off quickly towards home, as though he knew that old Farmer Evans was laid up with rheumatism, and that his wife wished to get back to him as soon as possible.

A Bit of Bala Lake.

CHAPTER IV.

TWO MILES TO A BIBLE.

'Tis written, man shall not live alone,
    By the perishing bread of earth;
Thou givest the soul a richer food
    To nourish the heavenly birth.
And yet to our fields of golden grain
    Thou bringest the harvest morn;
Thine op'ning hand is the life of all,
    For Thou preparest them corn.

R. EVANS'S farm was a curious old-fashioned place. The house was a large, rambling building, with many queer ups and downs, and with oddly-shaped windows in all sorts of unexpected places. And yet there was an aspect of homely comfort about the house not always to be found in far finer and more imposing-looking residences. At the back were the out-buildings—the sheds and cow-houses, the poultry-pen, the stables and pig-sties; while stretching away beyond these again were the home paddock, the drying-ground, and a small enclosed field, which went by the name of Hospital Meadow, on account of its being used for disabled animals that needed a rest.

With the farmer himself we made acquaintance two years ago at the meeting, when he spoke so kindly to Mary; and he was still the same good, honest, industrious, God-fearing man, never forgetting in the claims and anxieties of his work, what he owed to the Giver of all, who sends His rain for the watering of the seed, and His sun for the ripening of the harvest.

Nor did he—as too many farmers are in

the habit of doing—repine at Providence, and find fault with God's dealings if the rain came down upon the hay before it was safely carried, or if an early autumn gale laid his wheat even with the earth from which it sprang, ere the sickle could be put into it. Nor did he complain and grumble even when disease showed itself among the breed of small but active cattle of which he was justly proud, and carried off besides some of his fine sheep, destined for the famous Welsh mutton which sometimes is to be found on English tables.

In short, he was contented with what the Lord sent, and said with Job, when a misfortune occurred, " Shall we receive good at the hands of the Lord, and shall we not receive evil ? "

Of Mrs. Evans we have already spoken, and if we add here that she was a true helpmeet to her husband, in matters both temporal and spiritual, that is all we need say in her praise.

This worthy couple had three children. The eldest was already grown up ; she was a fine girl, and a great comfort and help to her mother. The younger children were boys, who went to a grammar school in a town a mile or two away : they were manly, high-spirited little fellows, well-trained, and as honest and true as their parents.

Such, then, was the family into which our little Mary was welcomed with all love and kindness. She was shy and timid the first time, for the farm-house was a much finer place than any home she had hitherto seen ; and there was an atmosphere of warmth, and there were delicious signs of plenty, which were unknown in Jacob Jones's poor little cottage, where everything was upon the most frugal, not to say meagre, scale.

But Mary's shyness did not last long ; indeed it disappeared wholly soon after she had crossed the threshold, where she was met by Mrs. Evans with a hearty welcome and a motherly kiss.

"Come in, little one," said the good woman, drawing her into the cosy, old-fashioned kitchen, where a kettle was singing on the hob, and an enticing fragrance of currant shortcake, baking for an early tea, scented the air.

"There, get warm, dear," said Mrs. Evans, "and then you shall go to the parlour, and study the Bible. And have you got a pencil and scrap of paper to take notes if you want them?"

"Yes, thank you, ma'am, I brought them with me," replied Mary.

For a few minutes she sat there, basking in the pleasant, cheery glow of the fire-light; then she was admitted to the parlour, where, on the table in the centre of the room, and covered reverently with a clean white cloth, was the precious book.

It must not be thought from the care thus taken of it that the Bible was never used. On the contrary, it was always read at prayers night and morning; and the farmer, whenever he had a spare half-hour, liked nothing better than to study the sacred book, and seek to understand its teachings.

" There's no need to tell you to be careful of our Bible, and to turn over the leaves gently, Mary, I'm sure," said Mrs. Evans ; " you would do that anyway, I know. And now, my child, I'll leave you and the Bible together. When you've learned your lesson for Sunday school, and read all you want, come back into the kitchen and have some tea before you go."

Then the good farmer's wife went away, leaving Mary alone with a Bible for the first time in her life.

Presently the child raised the napkin, and, folding it neatly, laid it on one side.

Then, with trembling hands, she opened the book, opened it at the fifth chapter of John, and her eyes caught these words, " Search the scriptures ; for in them ye think ye have eternal life : and they are they which testify of Me."

" I will! I will!" she cried, feeling as if
the words were spoken directly to her by
some Divine voice. " I will search and learn
all I can. Oh, if I had but a Bible of my
own!" And this wish, this sigh for the
rare and coveted treasure, was the key-note
to a grand chorus of glorious harmony
which, years after, spread in volume, until
it rolled in waves of sound over the whole
earth. Yes, that yearning in a poor child's
heart was destined to be a means of light
and knowledge to millions of souls in the
future. Thus verily has God often chosen
the weak things of the world to carry out
His great designs, and work His will. And
here, once more, is an instance of the small
beginnings which have great results—results
whose importance is not to be calculated on
this side of eternity.

When Mary had finished studying the
Scripture lesson for the morrow, and had
enjoyed a plentiful meal in the cosy kitchen,
she said good-bye to her kind friends, and

set off on her homeward journey, her mind full of the one great longing, out of which a resolution was slowly shaping itself.

It was formed at last.

" I *must* have a Bible of my own ! " she said aloud, in the earnestness of her purpose. " I must have one, if I save up for it for ten years ! " and by the time this was settled in her mind the child had reached her home.

Christmas had come, and with it some holidays for Mary and the other scholars who attended the school at Abergynolwyn ; but our little heroine would only have been sorry for the cessation of lessons, had it not been that during the holidays she had determined to commence carrying out her plan of earning something towards the purchase of a Bible.

Without neglecting her home duties, she managed to undertake little jobs of work, for which the neighbours were glad to give her a trifle. Now it was to mind a baby while the mother was at the wash-tub. Now to pick up sticks and brushwood in the woods for fuel; or to help to mend and patch the poor garments of the family for a worn, weary mother, who was thankful to give a small sum for this timely welcome help.

And every halfpenny, every farthing (and farthings were no unusual fee among such poor people as those of whom we are telling) was put into a rough little money-box which Jacob made for the purpose, with a hole in the lid. The box was kept in a cupboard, on a shelf where Mary could reach it, and it was a real and heartfelt joy to her when she could bring her day's earnings—some little copper coins, perhaps—and drop them in, longing for the time to come when they would have swelled to the requisite sum—a large sum unfortunately—for buying a Bible.

It was about this time that good Mrs. Evans, knowing the child's earnest wish, and wanting to encourage and help her, made her the present of a fine cock and two hens.

"Nay, nay, my dear, don't thank me," said she, when Mary was trying to tell her how grateful she was; "I've done it, first to help you along with that Bible you've set your heart on, and then, too, because I love you, and like to give you pleasure. So now, my child, when the hens begin to lay, which will be early in the spring, you can sell your eggs, for these will be your very own to do what you like with, and you can put the money to any use you please. I think I know what you'll do with it," added Mrs. Evans, with a smile.

But the first piece of silver that Mary had the satisfaction of dropping into her box was earned before she had any eggs to sell, and in quite a different way from the sums which she had hitherto received. She was walking one evening along the road from Towyn, whither she had been sent on an errand for her father, when her foot struck against some object lying in the road; and, stooping to pick it up, she found it was a large leather purse. Wondering whose it could be, the child went on, until, while still within half a mile from home, she met a man walking slowly, and evidently searching for something. He looked up as Mary approached, and she recognized him as Farmer Greaves, a brother-in-law of Mrs. Evans.

"Ah! good evening, Mary Jones," said he; "I've had such a loss! Coming home from market I dropped my purse, and——"

"I've just found a purse, sir," said Mary; "is this it?"

"You've found a purse?" exclaimed the farmer, eagerly. "Yes, indeed, my dear, that is mine, and I'm very much obliged to you. No, stay a moment," he called after her, for Mary was already trudging off again. "I should like to give you a trifle for your hon—— I mean just some trifle by way of thanks."

As he spoke, his finger and thumb closed on a bright shilling, which surely would not have been too much to give to a poor child who had found a heavy purse. But he thought better (or worse) of it, and took out instead a sixpence and handed it to Mary, who took it with very heartfelt thanks, and ran home as quickly as possible to drop her silver treasure safely into the box, where it was destined to keep its poorer brethren company for many a long year.

But the Christmas holidays were soon over, and then it was difficult for Mary to keep up with her daily lessons, and her Sunday-school tasks, the latter involving the weekly visits to the farm-house for the study of the Bible. What with these and her home duties, sometimes weeks passed without her having time to earn a penny towards the purchase of the sacred treasure.

Sometimes, too, she was rather late in reaching home on the Saturday evenings, and now and again Molly was uneasy about her. For Mary would come by short cuts over the hills, along ways which, however

safe in the daytime, were rough and un-
pleasant, if not dangerous, after dark; and
in these long winter evenings the daylight
vanished very early.

It was on one of these occasions that
Molly and Jacob Jones were sitting and
waiting for their daughter.

The old clock had already struck
eight. She had never been so late as
this before.

"Our Molly ought to be home, Jacob,"
said Molly, breaking a silence disturbed
only by the noise of Jacob's busy loom.
"It's got as dark as dark, and there's no
moon to-night. The way's a rugged one,
if she comes the short cut across the hill,
and she's not one to choose a long road if
she can find a shorter, bless her! She's more
than after her time. I hope no harm's come
to the child," and Molly walked to the
window and looked out.

"Don't be fretting yourself, Molly," replied
Jacob, pausing in his work; "Mary's out on

a good errand, and He who put the love of good things in her heart will take care of her in her going out and in her coming in, from henceforth, even for evermore."

Jacob spoke solemnly, but with a tone of conviction that comforted his wife, as words of his had often done before ; and just then a light step bounded up to the door, the latch was lifted, and Mary's lithe young figure entered the cottage, her dark eyes shining with intelligence, her cheeks flushed with exercise, a look of eager animation overspreading the whole of her bright face and seeming to diffuse a radiance round the cottage, while it shone reflected in the countenances of Jacob and Molly.

"Well, child, what have you learned to-day?" questioned Jacob. "Have you studied your lesson for the Sunday school ? "

" Ay, father, that I have, and a beautiful lesson it was," responded the child. " It was the lesson and Mr. Evans together that kept me so late."

" How so, Mary?" asked Molly. "We've been right down uneasy about you, fearing lest something had happened to you."

"You needn't have been so, mother dear," replied the little girl, with something of her father's quiet assurance. "God knew what I was about, and He would not let any harm come to me. Oh, father, the more I read about Him the more I want to know, and I shall never rest until I've a Bible of my own. But to-day I've brought home a big bit of the farmer's Bible with me."

"What do you mean, Mary? How could you do such a thing?" questioned Molly in amazement.

"Only in my head, mother dear, of course," replied the child ; then in a lower voice she added, "*and my heart.*"

"And what is the bit ?" asked Jacob.

"It's the seventh chapter of Matthew," said Mary. "Our Sunday lesson was from the first verse to the end of the twelfth verse.

But it was so easy and so beautiful, that I went on and on, till I'd learned the whole chapter. And just as I had finished, Mr. Evans came in and asked me if I understood it all ; and when I said there were some bits that puzzled me, he was so kind and explained them. If you like, mother and father, I'll repeat you the chapter."

So Jacob pushed away his work, and took his old seat in the chimney corner, and Molly began some knitting, while Mary sat down on a stool at her father's feet, and beginning at the first verse, repeated the whole chapter without a single mistake, without a moment's hesitation, and with a tone and emphasis which showed her comprehension of the truths so beautifully taught, and her sympathy with them.

" Mark my words, wife," said Jacob that night, when Mary had gone to bed, "that child will do a work for the Lord before she dies. See you not how He Himself is leading and guiding His lamb into green pastures and beside still waters? Why, Molly, when she repeated that verse, 'Ask, and ye shall receive,' I saw her eyes shine, and her cheeks glow again, and I knew she was thinking of the Bible that she's set her heart on, and which I doubt not she's praying for often enough when we know nothing about it. And the Lord He will give it her some day. Of that I'm moral certain. Yes, Molly, our Mary will have her Bible!"

" The Word of the Lord endureth for ever."
From a Bible in the Society's Library (C. Barker, 1585).

CHAPTER V.

FAITHFUL IN THAT WHICH IS LEAST.

Since this one talent Thou hast granted me,
I give Thee thanks, and joy, in blessing Thee,
    That I am worthy any.
I would not hide or bury it, but rather
Use it for Thee and Thine, O Lord and Father,
    And make one talent many.

E may be sure that various were the influences tending to mould the character of Mary Jones during the years of her school-life, confirming in her the wonderful steadfastness of purpose and earnestness of spirit for which she was remarkable, as well

as fostering the tender and loving nature that made her beloved by all with whom she had to do.

Her master, John Ellis (who afterwards was stationed at Barmouth), seems to have been a conscientious and able teacher, and we may infer that he took no small part in the development of the mind and heart of a pupil who must always have been an object of special interest from her great intelligence and eagerness to learn.

But as the years passed, the time came for John Ellis to change his sphere of labour. He did so, and his place was taken by a man, a sketch of whose story may perhaps not inappropriately be given here, as that of the teacher under whom Mary Jones was being instructed at the time when a great event occurred in her history, an event the recounting of which we leave for the next chapter.

The successor to John Ellis was Lewis Williams, a man who from a low station in life, and from absolute ignorance, rose to a position of considerable influence and popularity; from an utterly heedless and godless life, to be a God-fearing and noble-minded Christian.

He was a man of small size, and from all that we can learn of his intellect and talents we can hardly think that they were of any high order. But what he lacked in mental gifts he made up in iron resolution, in a perseverance which was absolutely sublime in its determination not to be baffled.

He was born in Pennal in the year 1774; his parents were poor, but of them nothing further is known.

Like other boys at that time, and in that neighbourhood, he was wild and reckless, breaking the Sabbath continually, and otherwise drawing upon himself the censure of those with whom he was acquainted.

But when he was about eighteen years old he chanced on one occasion to be at a prayer-meeting, when a Mr. Jones, of Mathafarn, was reading and expounding the fifth chapter of the Epistle to the Romans.

The word of God, thus made known to Lewis Williams in perhaps a fresh and striking manner, was the means of carrying home to his hitherto hard heart the conviction of sin ; and a change was from that time observed in him, which gradually deepened, until none could longer doubt that he had become an earnest and consistent Christian.

On the occasion of his requesting to be admitted to membership in a little Methodist church at Cwmllinian, he was asked (probably as one of the test questions), "If Jesus Christ asked you to do some work for Him, would you do it ?" His answer gives us the key to his success: "Oh yes; *whatever* Jesus required of me I would do *at once.*"

Such was the commencement of the religious life of this most singular man.

Some years after, when in service at a place called Trychiad, near Llanegryn, he could not but notice the ignorance of the boys in the neighbourhood, and, burning with zeal to perform some direct and special work for his Heavenly Master, he resolved to establish there a Sunday school, and a week-night school besides, if possible, in order to teach the lads to read.

This would have been praiseworthy, but still nothing remarkable in the way of an undertaking, had Lewis Williams received any sort of education himself. But as he had never enjoyed a day's schooling in his life, and could hardly read a word correctly, the thought of teaching others seemed, to say the least, rather a wild idea.

But how often the old proverb has been proved true, that where there is a will there is a way ; and once more was this verified in the experience of Lewis Williams.

Owing to the young man's untiring energy and courage, his school was opened in a short time, and he began the work of instruction, teaching, we are told, the alphabet to the lowest class by setting it to the tune of " The March of the Men of Harlech,"

Dr. Moffat, we know, tried the same plan of melody lessons forty years later, with a number of Bechuana children, teaching them their letters to the tune of "Auld Lang Syne" with wonderful facility and success.

But Lewis Williams, if he set up for a schoolmaster at all, could hardly confine his instructions to the lowest class in the school ; yet in undertaking the teaching of the older boys, he was coming face to face with an obstacle which might well have seemed insurmountable to any one whose will was less strong or courage less undaunted.

The master could not read, or at least he could neither read fluently nor correctly, yet he had bound himself to teach reading to the lads in his school.

Painfully mindful of his deficiencies, he used, before commencing his Sunday-school exercises or his evening classes, to pay a visit to a good woman, Betty Evans by name, who had learned to read well. Under her tuition he prepared the lessons he was

going to give that day or the next, so that
in reality the master of that flourishing little
school was only beforehand with his scholars
by a few hours.

At other times he would invite a number
of scholars from an endowed high school in
the neighbourhood, to come for reading and
argument.

With quiet tact and careful foresight he
would arrange that the subject taken for
reading and discussion should include the
lesson which he would shortly have to give.

While the reading and talk went on, he
listened with rapt attention. The discussions as to the meaning or pronunciation of
the more difficult words was all clear gain to
him, as familiarizing his mind with what he
desired to know.

But none of these youths meeting thus
had an inkling that the man who invited
them, who spoke so discreetly, and listened
so attentively, was himself a learner, and
dependent upon them for the proper con-

struction of phrases, or for the correct pronunciation of words occurring in his next day's or week's lessons.

The school duties were always commenced with prayer, and as the master had a restless, unruly set of lads to do with, he invented a somewhat peculiar way of securing their attention for the devotions in which he led them.

Familiar with military exercises through former experiences in the militia, he would put the restless boys through a series of these, and when they came to " stand at ease," and "attention!" he would at once, but very briefly and simply, engage in prayer.

While Lewis Williams was thus hard at work at Llanegryn, seeking to win hearts to the Saviour, and train minds to serve Him, it happened that Mr. Charles of Bala, intending to preside at a members' meeting to be held at Abergynolwyn, arrived at Bryncrug the evening before, and spent the night at the house of John Jones, the schoolmaster of that place.

In the course of conversation with his host, Mr. Charles asked him if he knew of a suitable person to undertake the charge of one of his recently established schools in the neighbourhood. John Jones replied that he had heard of a young man at Llanegryn, who taught the children both on week-nights and Sundays ; " but," added the schoolmaster, " as I hear that he himself cannot read, I can hardly understand how he is able to instruct others."

" Impossible ! " exclaimed Mr. Charles. " How can any one teach what he does not himself know ? "

" Still, they say he does so," replied John Jones.

Mr. Charles at once expressed a wish to see this mysterious instructor of youth, who was reported as imparting to others what he did not himself possess. The next day, accordingly, summoned by John Jones, our young schoolmaster made his appearance. His rustic garb, and the simplicity of his manner, gave the impression of his being anything but a pedagogue, whatever might have been said of him.

" Well, my young friend," said Mr. Charles, in the genial pleasant way that was natural to him, and that at once inspired with confidence all with whom he had to do, " they tell me you keep a school at Llanegryn yonder, on Sundays and week-nights, for the purpose of teaching children to read. Have you many scholars ? "

" Yes, sir, far more than I am able to teach," replied Lewis Williams.

" And do they learn a little by your teaching ? " asked Mr. Charles, as kindly as ever, but with a quaint smile lurking round his mouth.

" I think some of them learn, sir," responded the young teacher, very modestly, and with an overwhelming sense of his own ignorance — a consciousness that showed itself painfully both in his voice and manner

"Do you understand any English?" questioned Mr. Charles.

"Only a stray word or two, sir, which I picked up when serving in the militia."

"Do you read Welsh fluently?"

"No, sir, I can read but little, but I am doing my very best to learn."

"Were you at a school before beginning to teach?" asked Mr. Charles, more and more interested in the young man who stood so meekly before him.

"No, sir. I never had a day's schooling in my life."

"And your parents did not teach you to read while you were at home?"

"No, sir, my parents could not read a word for themselves."

Mr. Charles opened his Bible at the first chapter of the Epistle to the Hebrews, and asked Lewis Williams to read the opening verses.

Slowly, hesitatingly, and with several mistakes, the young man complied, stumbling with difficulty through the first verse.

" That will do, my lad," said Mr. Charles ; " but how you are able to teach others to read, passes my comprehension. Tell me now by what plan you instruct the children."

Then the poor young teacher described the methods to which he had recourse for receiving and imparting instruction ; he gave an account of his musical A B C ; the lessons given to himself by Betty Evans ; the readings and discussions of the grammar-school boys ; and the scholars playing at " little soldiers."

As Lewis Williams proceeded with his confessions (for such they appeared to him), Mr. Charles, with the discernment which seems to have been one of his characteristics, had penetrated through the roughness and uncouthness of the narrator to the real force of character and earnestness of the man. He saw that this humble follower of the Saviour had earnestly endeavoured to improve his one talent, and work with it in the Master's service, and that he only needed help in the development of his capacity, to render him a most valuable servant of Christ.   He recommended him therefore to place himself for a time under the tuition of John Jones, and thus fit himself for efficient teaching in his turn.

During the following three months, Lewis Williams followed the advice of Mr. Charles ; and this was all the schooling that he ever had.

His self-culture did not, however, cease with the help gained from John Jones. Every hour he could spare was devoted to study, in order to fit himself for one of the schoolmasters' places under Mr. Charles's special control and management.   And we are told that in order to perfect himself further in reading, he used to visit neighbouring churches, to study the delivery and reading of the ministers presiding there.

His earnest desire was gratified at last, for in the year 1799—that is, when he was about twenty-five years of age—he was engaged by Mr. Charles as a paid teacher in one of his schools. He was removed to Abergynolwyn a year later, and here, among his pupils, was our young friend Mary Jones.

In his subsequent years of work he was the means of establishing many new schools, and of reviving others which were losing their vitality ; and at length he even became a preacher, so great was his zeal in his Master's service, and so anxious was he that all should know the truth and join in the work of the Lord.

He died in his eighty-eighth year, followed by the sincere gratitude and deep love of the many whom he had benefited.

Our story now returns to Mary Jones, who at the time that Lewis Williams became schoolmaster at Abergynolwyn, was nearly sixteen years old.

She was an active, healthy maiden, full of

life and energy, as earnest and as diligent as ever. Nor had her purpose faltered for one moment as regarded the purchase of a Bible. Through six long years she had hoarded every penny, denying herself the little indulgences which the poverty of her life must have made doubly attractive to one so young. She had continued her visits to the farm-house, and while she there studied her Bible lessons for school, her desire to possess God's Holy Book for herself grew almost to a passion.

What joy it would be, she often thought, if every day she could read and commit to memory portions of Scripture, storing her mind and heart with immortal truths. "But the time will come," she had added, "when I shall have my Bible. Yes, though I have waited so long, the time will come." Then on her knees beside her little bed she had prayed aloud, "Dear Lord, let the time come quickly!"

As may be supposed, Mary was the great

pride and delight of her parents. She was more useful, more her mother's right hand than ever; and her father, as he looked into her clear, honest, intelligent dark eyes, and heard her recite her lesson for school, or recount for his benefit all the explanations to which she had that day listened, thanked the Lord in his heart, for his brave, God-fearing child, and prayed that she might grow up to be a blessing to all with whom she might have to do in the future.

" If a man love me, he will keep my words."
Tail-piece from Coverdale's New Test. (1538) *in the Society's Library.*

CHAPTER VI.

ON THE WAY.

A strong, brave heart, and a purpose true,
  Are better than wealth untold,
Planting a garden in barren ways,
  And turning their dust to gold.

 MOTHER! O father! only think! Mrs. Evans has just paid me for that work I did for her, and it is more than I expected; and now I find I have enough to buy a Bible. I'm so happy I don't know what to do."

Mary had just come from the farm-house, and now as she bounded in with the joyful news, Jacob stopped his loom, and held out both hands.

"Is it really so, Mary? After six years' saving! Nay then, God be thanked, child, who first put the wish into your heart, and then gave you patience to wait and work to get the thing you wanted. Bless you, my little maid," and Jacob laid a hand solemnly upon his daughter's head, adding in a lower tone, "and she shall be blest!"

"But tell me, father dear," said Mary after a little pause, "where am I to buy the Bible? There are no Bibles to be had here or at Abergynolwyn."

"I cannot tell you, Mary, but our preacher, William Huw, will know," replied Jacob; "you will do well to go to him to-morrow, and ask how you're to get the book."

Acting upon her father's suggestion, Mary accordingly went the next day to Llechwedd to William Huw, and to him she put the question so all-important to her. But he replied that not a copy could be obtained (even of the Welsh version published the year before) nearer than of Mr. Charles of

Bala ; and he added that he feared lest all the Bibles received by Mr. Charles from London had been sold or promised months ago.

This was discouraging news, and Mary went home, cast down indeed, but not in despair. There was still, she reflected, a chance that one copy of the Scriptures yet remained in Mr. Charles's possession ; and if so, that Bible should be hers.

The long distance —over twenty-five miles —the unknown road, the far-famed, but to her, strange minister, who was to grant her the boon she craved—all this, if it a little frightened her, did not for one moment threaten to change her purpose.

Even Jacob and Molly, who at first, on account of the distance, objected to her walking to Bala for the purchase of her Bible, ceased to oppose their will to hers ; "for," said good Jacob to his wife, "if it's the Lord answering our prayers and leading the child, as we prayed He might, it would ill become us to go against His wisdom."

And so our little Mary had her way, and having received permission for her journey, she went to a neighbour living near, and telling her of her proposed expedition, asked if she would lend her a wallet to carry home the treasure should she obtain it.

The neighbour, mindful of Mary's many little acts of thoughtful kindness towards herself and her children, and glad of any way in which she could show her grateful feeling and sympathy, put the wallet into the girl's hand, and bade her good-bye with a hearty "God speed you!"

The next morning, a fresh, breezy day in spring, in the year 1800, Mary rose almost as soon as it was light, and washed and dressed with unusual care; for was not this to be a day of days—the day for which she had waited for years, and which must, she thought, make her the happiest of girls, or bring to her such grief and disappointment as she had never yet known?

Her one pair of shoes—far too precious a

possession to be worn on a twenty-five mile walk—Mary placed in her wallet, intending to put them on as soon as she reached the town.

Early as was the hour, Molly and Jacob were both up to give Mary her breakfast of hot milk and bread, and have family prayer, offering a special petition for God's blessing on their child's undertaking, and for His protection and care during her journey.

This fortified and comforted Mary, and, kissing her parents, she went out into the dawn of that lovely day—a day which lived in her remembrance till the last hour of her long and useful life.

She set out at a good pace—not too quick, for that would have wearied her ere a quarter of her journey could be accomplished, but an even, steady walk, her bare brown feet treading lightly but firmly along the road, her head erect, her clear eyes glistening, her cheek with a healthy flush under the brown skin. So she went—the bonniest, blithest maiden on that sweet spring morning in all the country round. Never before had every-

CADER IDRIS.

thing about her looked to Mary as it looked on
that memorable morning. The dear old moun-

tain seemed to gaze down protectingly upon her The very sun, as it came up on the eastern horizon, appeared to have a smile specially for her. The larks soared from the meadow till their trilling died away in the sky, like a tuneful prayer sent up to God. The rabbits peeped out at her from leafy nooks and holes, and even a squirrel, as it ran up a tree, stopped to glance familiarly at our little maiden, as much as to say, "Good morning, Mary; good luck to you!" And the girl's heart was attuned to the blithe loveliness of nature, full of thankfulness for the past and of hope for the future.

And now, leaving our heroine bravely wending her way towards Bala, we will just record briefly the history of that good and earnest man on whom the child's hopes and expectations were this day fixed, and who therefore, in Mary's eyes, must be the greatest and most important person—for the time—in the world.

But apart from the ideas and opinions of

a simple girl, Thomas Charles of Bala was in reality a person of great influence and high standing in Wales, and had been instrumental in the organization and execution of much important and excellent work, in places where ignorance and darkness had hitherto prevailed. Hence the name (by which he often went) of "the Apostolic Charles of Bala."

He was now about fifty years of age, and had spent twenty years in going about among the wildest parts of Wales, preaching the Word of Life, forming schools, and using his great and varied talents wholly in the service of his Master.

At the age of eighteen he had given himself to the Saviour, and his first work for the Lord was in his own home, where he was the means of instituting family worship and exerting an influence for good none the less powerful that it was loving and gentle.

His education was begun at Carmarthen, and continued at Oxford, and we learn that the Rev. John Newton was a kind and good friend to him during a part of his student life, and that on one occasion his vacation was spent at the house of this excellent man.

The Rev. Thomas Charles became an ordained minister of the Church of England in due course, but owing to the faithful and outspoken style of his preaching, many of his own denomination took offence and would not receive him ; so he seceded from the Church of England and joined the Welsh Calvinistic Methodists ; but his greatest work hitherto had been the establishment of Day and Sunday Schools in Wales. The organization of these, the selection of paid teachers, the periodical visiting and examination of the various schools, made Mr. Charles's life a very busy one. But as he toiled on, he could see that his labour was not in vain. Wherever he went, carrying the good news, proving it in his life, spending all he was and all he had in the service of Christ,—the darkness that hung over the people lifted, and the true light began to shine.

The ignorance and immorality gave place to a desire for knowledge and holiness, and the soil that was barren and stony became the planting-place of sweet flowers and pleasant fruits.

Such, in brief, was the man—and such his work up to the time of Mary Jones's journey to Bala.

About the middle of the day Mary stopped to rest and to eat some food which her mother had provided for her. Under a tree in a grassy hollow not far from the road, she half reclined, protected from the sun by the tender green of the spring foliage, and cooling her hot dusty feet in the soft damp grass that spread like a velvet carpet all over the hollow.

Ere long too she spied a little stream, trickling down a hill on its way to the sea, and here she drank, and washed her face and hands and feet, and was refreshed.

Half an hour's quiet rested her thoroughly,

then she jumped up, slung her wallet over
her shoulder again, and recommenced her
journey

The rest of the way, along a dusty road
for the most part, and under a warm sun, was
fatiguing enough ; but the little maiden
plodded patiently on, though her feet were
blistered and cut with the stones, and her
head ached and her limbs were very weary.

Once a kind cottager, as she passed, gave
her a drink of butter-milk, and a farmer's
little daughter, as Mary neared her destina-
tion, offered her a share of the supper she
was eating as she sat in the porch in the cool
of the evening ; but these were all the adven-
tures or incidents in Mary's journey till she
got to Bala.

On arriving there, she followed out the
instructions that had been given her by
William Huw, and went to the house of
David Edwards, a much respected Methodist
preacher at Bala.

This good man received her most kindly,

questioned her as to her motive in coming so far, but ended by telling her that owing to Mr. Charles's early and regular habits (one secret of the large amount of work which he accomplished), it was now too late in the day to see him.

" But," added the kind old man, seeing his young visitor's disappointment, " you shall sleep here to-night, and we will go to Mr. Charles's as soon as I see light in his study-window to-morrow morning, so that you may accomplish your errand in good time, and be able to reach home before night."

With grateful thanks Mary accepted the hospitality offered her, and after a simple supper, she was shown into the little prophet's chamber where she was to sleep.

There, after repeating a chapter of the Bible, and offering an earnest prayer, she lay down, her mind and body alike resting, her faith sure that her journey would not be in vain, but that He who had led her safely thus far, would give her her heart's desire.

And the curtains of night fell softly about the good preacher's humble dwelling, shadowing the sleepers there ; and the rest of those sleepers was sweet, and their safety assured, for watching over them was the God of the night and the day—the God whom they loved and trusted, and underneath them were the Everlasting Arms.

A CORNER OF BALA LAKE.

BALA.

CHAPTER VII.

TEARS THAT PREVAIL.

Often tears of joy and sorrow meet ;
Marah's bitter waters turn'd to sweet.

BALA is even now a quiet little town,
situated near the end of Bala Lake, on

the north side of a wide, cultivated valley.
A hundred years ago, it was more quiet and
rural still. The scenery is pastoral in its
character, hilly rather than mountainous, but
well wooded and watered. The town is a
favourite resort of people fond of shooting
and fishing. Altogether it is a pretty, cheer-
ful, healthy spot, but wanting in the imposing
grandeur and rugged beauty of many other
parts of North Wales.

Such, then, was the place to which our little
heroine's weary feet had brought her on the
preceding evening, and such was the home
—for the greater part of his life—of Thomas
Charles of Bala.

Mary's deep, dreamless sleep was not
broken until her host knocked at her door
at early dawning.

"Wake up, Mary Jones, my child! Mr.
Charles is an early riser, and will soon be at
work. The dawn is breaking ; get up, dear !"

Mary started up, rubbing her eyes. The
time had really come, then, and in a few

BALA LAKE.

minutes she would know what was to be the result of her long waiting.

Her heart beat quicker as she washed and dressed, but her excitement calmed when she sat down for a minute or two on the side of her bed, and repeated the 23rd Psalm.

The sweet words of the royal singer were the first that occurred to her, and now, as she murmured " The Lord is my shepherd, I shall not want," she felt as though she were of a truth being watched over and cared for by a loving Shepherd, and being led by Him.

She was soon ready, and David Edwards and his guest proceeded together to Mr. Charles's house.

" There's a light in his study," said the good old preacher. " Our apostle is at his desk already. There are not many like him, Mary ; always at work for the Master The world would be better had we more such men."

Mary did not reply, but she listened intently as David Edwards knocked at the door. There was no answer, only the tread of a foot across the floor above, and the next moment the door opened, and Mr. Charles himself stood before them.

"Good morning, friend Edwards! And what brings you here so early? Come in, do," said the genial, hearty voice, which so many knew, and had cause to love. Then, as David Edwards entered, Mr. Charles noticed the little figure behind him in the doorway.

A rather timid shrinking little figure it was now, for Mary's courage was fast ebbing away, and she felt shy and frightened.

A few words of explanation passed between the old preacher and Mr. Charles; then Mary was invited to enter the study.

"Now, my child," said Mr. Charles, "don't be afraid, but tell me all about yourself, where you live, and what your name is, and what you want."

At this Mary took courage and answered all Mr Charles's questions, her voice (which at first was low and tremulous) strengthening as her courage returned. She told him all about her home and her parents, her longing when quite a child for a Bible of her own, then of the long years during which she had saved up her little earnings towards the purchase of a Bible—the sum being now complete.

Then Mr. Charles examined her as to her Scripture knowledge, and was delighted with the girl's intelligent replies, which showed how earnestly and thoroughly she had studied the Book she loved so well.

" But how, my child," said he, " did you get to know the Bible as you do, when you did not own one for yourself? "

Then Mary told him of the visits to the farm-house, and how, through the kindness of the farmer and his wife, she had been able to study her Sunday-school lessons, and commit portions of Scripture to memory.

As she informed Mr. Charles of all that had taken place, and he began to realize how brave, and patient, and earnest, and hopeful she had been through all these years of waiting, and how far she had now

come to obtain possession of the coveted
treasure, his bright face became over-
shadowed, and, turning to David Edwards,
he said, sadly, " I am indeed grieved that
this dear girl should have come all the way
from Llanfihangel to buy a Bible, and that
I should be unable to supply her with one.
The consignment of Welsh Bibles that I
received from London last year was all
sold out months ago, excepting a few copies
which I have kept for friends whom I must
not disappoint. Unfortunately the Society
which has hitherto supplied Wales with the
Scriptures declines to print any more, and
where to get Welsh Bibles to satisfy our
country's need I know not."

Until now, Mary had been looking up
into Mr. Charles's face, with her great, dark
eyes full of hope and confidence ; but as he
spoke these words to David Edwards, and
she noticed his overclouded face, and began
to understand the full import of his words,
the room seemed to her to darken suddenly,

and, dropping into the nearest seat, she buried her face in her hands, and sobbed as, perhaps, few girls of her age had ever sobbed before.

It was all over, then, she said to herself —all of no use—the prayers, the longing, the waiting, the working, the saving for six long years, the weary tramp with bare feet, the near prospect of her hopes being fulfilled, all, all in vain! And to a mind so stocked with Bible texts as hers, the language of the Psalmist seemed the natural outburst for so great a grief, "Hath God forgotten to be gracious? Hath He in anger shut up His tender mercies?" All in vain—all of no use! And the poor little head, lately so erect, drooped lower and lower, and the sunburnt hands, roughened by work and exposure, could not hide the great hot tears that rolled down, chasing each other over cheeks out of which the accustomed rosy tint had fled, and falling unheeded through her fingers.

There were a few moments during which only Mary's sobs broke the silence ; but those sobs had appealed to Mr. Charles's heart with a pathos which he was wholly unable to resist.

With his own voice broken and unsteady, he said, as he rose from his seat, and laid a hand on the drooping head of the girl before him :

" My dear child, I see you *must* have a Bible, difficult as it is for me to spare you one. It is impossible, yes, simply impossible, to refuse you."

In the sudden revulsion of feeling that followed these words, Mary could not speak ; but she glanced up with such a face of mingled rain and sunshine—such a rainbow smile— such a look of inexpressible joy and thankfulness in her brimming eyes, that the responsive tears gushed to the eyes of both Mr. Charles and David Edwards.

Mr. Charles turned away for a moment to a book-cupboard that stood behind him, and opening it, he drew forth a Bible.

Then, laying a hand once more on Mary's

head, with the other he placed the Bible in her grasp, and, looking down the while into the earnest, glistening eyes upturned to him, he said :

" If you, my dear girl, are glad to receive this Bible, truly glad am I to be able to give it to you. Read it carefully, study it diligently, treasure up the sacred words in your memory, and act up to its teachings."

And then, as Mary, quite overcome with delight and thankfulness, began once more to sob, but softly, and with sweet, happy tears, Mr. Charles turned to the old preacher, and said, huskily, " David Edwards, is not such a sight as this enough to melt the hardest heart ? A girl, so young, so poor, so intelligent, so familiar with Scripture, compelled to walk all the distance from Llanfihangel to Bala (about fifty miles there and back) to get a Bible! From this day I can never rest until I find out some means of supplying the pressing wants of my country that cries out for the Word of God."

MR. CHARLES'S HOUSE AT BALA.

Half an hour later, Mary Jones, having shared David Edwards's frugal breakfast, set off on her homeward journey.

The day was somewhat cloudy, but the child did not notice it ; her heart was full of sunshine. The wind blew strongly, but a great calm was in her soul, and her young face was so full of happiness that the simple folk she met on the way could not but notice her as she tripped blithely on, her bare feet seeming hardly to press the ground, her eyes shining with deep content, while the wallet containing her newly-found treasure was no longer slung across her back, but clasped close to her bosom.

The sun rose and burst through the clouds, glorifying all the landscape ; and onward steadily went Mary, her heart, like the lark's song, full of thanksgiving, and her voice breaking out now and again into melody, to which the words of some old hymn or of a well-known and much-loved text set themselves, without an effort on the girl's part.

On, still on, she went, heeding not the length and weariness of the way; and the afternoon came, and the sun set in the western heavens with a glory that made Mary think of the home prepared above for God's children; that heaven with its walls of jasper, and its gates of pearl, and its streets of gold, and its light that needs nor sun nor moon, but streams from the Life-giving Presence of God Himself.

That evening Jacob and his wife were seated waiting for supper and for Mary. What news would the child bring? How had she sped? Had she received her Bible? These were some of the questions which the anxious parents asked themselves, listening the while for their daughter's return after the fatigues and possible dangers of her fifty miles' walk.

But the worthy couple were not long kept in suspense.

Presently the light step which they knew so well, approached the cottage; the latch was lifted, and Mary entered, weary, foot-sore, dusty and travel-stained indeed, but with happiness dimpling her cheeks and flashing in her eyes. And Jacob held out both arms to his darling, and as he clasped her to his heart, he murmured in the words of the prophet of old, " Is it well with the child ? " and Mary, from the depths of a satisfied heart, answered solemnly, but with gladness, " It is well."

We sometimes see—and particularly in the case of young people—that great eagerness for the possession of some coveted article is followed by indifference when the treasure is safely in their hands. It was not so, however, with Mary Jones The Bible for which she had toiled, and waited, and prayed, and wept, became each day more precious to her. The Word of the Lord was indeed nigh unto her, even in her mouth and in her heart.

Chapter after chapter was learned by heart, and the study of the Sunday-school lessons became her greatest privilege and delight.

If a question were asked by the teacher, which other girls could not answer, Mary was always appealed to, and was invariably ready with a thoughtful, intelligent reply, while in committing to memory not only chapters, but whole books of the Bible, she was unrivalled both in the school and neighbourhood.

Nor was this all. For though to love, and read, and learn the Bible are good things, this is not the sum of what is required by Him who has said "If ye love Me, *keep* My commandments."

Mary's study of the Word of God did not prevent the more than ever faithful discharge of all her duties. Her mother, who had at one time feared that Mary's desire for book learning, and longing to possess a Bible of her own, might lead her to the neglect of her practical duties, was surprised and delighted to see that, although there was a change indeed in the girl, it was a change for the better.

The holy truths that sank into her heart, were but the precious seed in good ground, which brings forth fruit an hundredfold ; and the more entire the consecration of that young heart to the Lord, the sweeter became even the commonest duties of life, because they were done for Him.

Not very long after Mary's visit to Bala, she had the great pleasure of seeing again the kind friend with whom, in her memory, her beloved Bible would now always be associated.

Mr. Charles, in the course of his periodical visits to the various villages where his circulating schools were established, came to Abergynolwyn, to inspect the school there under the charge of Lewis Williams, and by examining the children personally, to assure himself of their progress.

Among the bright young faces upturned to him, his observant eye soon caught sight of one countenance that he had cause to remember with special and with deep interest ; and the interest deepened still more, when he found that from her alone all his most difficult questions received replies, and that her intelligence was only surpassed by the childlike humility which is one mark of the true Christian.

We may be very sure that Mr. Charles did not miss this opportunity of saying a few kind words to his young friend ; and that Mary in her turn treasured them up, and remembered them through the many years and the various events of her after-life.

BALA LAKE.

CHAPTER VIII.

THE WORK BEGUN.

Henceforward, then, the olive-leaf plucked off,
  Carried to every nation,
Shall promise be of re-awakening life,
  Our sinful world's salvation.

WE have seen that the incident recorded in the last chapter made a deep impression upon the mind and heart of Mr. Charles. The thought of that bare-footed child, her weary journey, her eagerness to spend her six

years' savings in the purchase of a Bible;
then her bitter tears of disappointment, and
her sweet tears of joy—all these came back
to his recollection again and again; came
blended with the memory of the ignorance
and darkness of too many of his countrymen,
and with the cry that was ascending all over
Wales for the Word of God.

The girl's story was only an illustration of
the terrible sense of spiritual death that prevailed during this famine of Bibles; and none
could know so well as this good man—whose
influence was, from the nature of his work,
very widely diffused—how deep a want lay
at the root of the people's degradation and
impiety, against which he seemed, with all his
earnest striving, to be making such slow progress. What wonder, then, that the question
how to secure the publication of sufficient
copies of God's Word for Wales, occupied his
mind almost without cessation?

In the winter of 1802, Mr. Charles visited
London, full of his one great thought and

purpose, though not as yet seeing how it was to be accomplished.

It was while revolving the matter in his mind one morning, that the idea occurred to him of a Society for the diffusion of the Scriptures, a society having for its sole object the publication and distribution of God's Holy Word.

Consulting with some of his friends who belonged to the Committee of the Religious Tract Society, he received the warmest sympathy and encouragement, and was introduced at their next meeting, where he spoke most feelingly and eloquently about Wales and its poverty in Bibles, bringing forward the story which forms the subject of our little book, and which gave point and pathos to his appeal on behalf of his countrymen.

Nor was the appeal without effect. A thrill of sympathy with a people that so longed and thirsted for the Word of God, ran through the assembled meeting. An earnest desire took possession of Mr.

Charles's hearers to do something towards supplying the great need which he so touchingly advocated; and the hearts of many were further stirred, and their sympathies quickened, when one of the secretaries of the Committee, the Reverend Joseph Hughes, rose, and in reply to Mr. Charles's appeal for Bibles for Wales, exclaimed enthusiastically : "Mr. Charles, surely a society might be formed for the purpose ; and if for Wales, why not for the world ?"

This noble Christian sentiment found an echo in the hearts of many among the audience, and the secretary was instructed to prepare a letter inviting Christians everywhere, and of all denominations, to unite in forming a society having for its object the diffusion of God's Word over the whole earth.

Two years passed in making known the purpose of the Committee, and in necessary preliminaries, but in the month of March, 1804, the British and Foreign Bible Society was actually established, and at its first meeting the sum of £700 was subscribed.

Unfortunately Mr. Charles was unable to be present at this meeting. He was hard at work at home in Wales, but he heard the news with the greatest joy ; and it was owing to his exertions and to those of his friends, as well as to the efforts of other Christian workers who deeply felt the great need of the people at this time, that the contributions in Wales amounted to nearly £1,900 ; most of this sum consisting of the subscriptions and donations of the lower and poorer classes.

In the foundation of the Bible Society all denominations met, and were brought thus into sympathy by a common cause, and an earnest wish to serve one common Master. Hence we see representatives of all Christian Churches working together for the good and enlightenment of the world.

Meanwhile, wherever Mr. Charles was at work, wherever his influence extended, there was awakened the longing, and thence arose

MONUMENT TO MR. CHARLES AT BALA.

the petition, for the Word of Life ; and wherever he told the story, either on Welsh or English platforms, of the little maiden of Llanfihangel, the simple narrative never failed to carry home some lessons to the heart of each hearer.

Great was the joy and thankfulness of this single-minded and hard-working minister of Christ, when he learnt that the first resolution of the Committee of the Bible Society was to bring out an edition of the Welsh Bible for the use of Welsh Sunday schools ; and his delight was greater still when the first consignment of these Bibles reached Bala in 1806.

Among the most useful workers in the early years of the Bible Society was the Reverend John Owen, who soon became one of its secretaries, and proved a most earnest and able promoter of the glorious enterprise.

Associated also with this time of the great Society's childhood are the honoured names of Steinkopff, of Wilberforce, and of

Josiah Pratt; while in Wales, among its earliest supporters, were Dr. Warren, Bishop of Bangor, and Dr. Burgess, Bishop of St. David's, who united cordially with Mr. Charles and others in the good work. As to Mr. Charles himself, he evinced the deepest interest in the new spheres of labour and usefulness opening in all directions,—an interest which showed itself in many practical ways up to the time of his death.

But in following the operations of the Bible Society, we must not forget our friend Mary Jones, who during this time had passed from early girlhood to womanhood.

On leaving school, she worked as a weaver, and we conclude that she was still living with her parents.

Of one thing we may be sure ; that her precious Bible was as dear to her as ever, and that she was intensely interested in the founding of the Bible Society, and in the news of the first edition of Welsh Bibles having been received at Bala.

But in addition to her weaving, and the household help she gave her mother, who was not so well or strong as formerly, Mary had developed a talent for dressmaking, which stood her in good stead when she wished to earn a little extra money.

All who could afford it came to her to cut out and make their dresses, and though Mary never wasted a moment, she sometimes found it quite difficult to do during the day all that she had planned.

As for Jacob, he was more and more a martyr to asthma, and when the winter winds and fogs came his sufferings were very great, though they never exceeded the quiet patience and fortitude with which he bore his affliction—bore it, as he said, "for the dear Lord's sake," who had borne so much for him.

Occasionally Mr. Charles would visit Abergynolwyn, and every now and then Llanfihangel, and at such times he and Mary Jones met again, and she would learn from him how the Society in London was going on—that great London which was a strange, distant, untried world to her, such vague ideas had she of its size and its distance from the little, quiet, secluded place where she lived.

And so, up in London, the great tree of life went on spreading, and growing, while the root from which it had sprung remained in Wales unperceived almost beneath the soil. And thus we see in this life that God has need of the high and the lowly, the great and the small, the gold and the baser metal; and *out* of all, and *through* all, and *in* all, He works His wondrous way, and permits His creatures to join, as it were, with Him in the turning of the world from darkness to His marvellous light.

(From a Bible in the Society's Library.)

LLAN-Y-CIL CHURCH.
(*The Burial-place of the Rev. Thomas Charles.*)

CHAPTER IX.

YOUTHFUL PROMISE FULFILLED.

Nurtured and nursed of Heaven, the blossom bloom'd,
    Until an open flower
With buds around it, gazed upon the sun,
    Or drank the shower ;
Nor did forget, in this the blooming time,
    The fragrance due
To Him who gives to Nature all her wealth,
    To flowers their hue.

WHEN next we glance at our heroine
of Llanfihangel, she is Mary Jones no

longer. A great change has come over her surroundings, and her school work and her old home life with her parents are things of the past. For she has married a weaver, Thomas Lewis by name, and is living at the village of Bryncrug, near Towyn, not very far from Llanfihangel. But the difference in circumstances has not changed the character of Mary, save as the advancing summer may be said to change the fruit by ripening it.

So dutiful and devoted a daughter as Mary had ever proved herself, would hardly have left her parents while she could minister to the wants of their declining years, work for them, and be their great joy and comfort. So it is only reasonable to suppose that ere she married, both good old Jacob and his wife had been laid to rest, and that Mary, in casting in her lot with Thomas Lewis, whom possibly she had known for many years, would be neglecting no duty that could be required from a loving daughter.

But here, at Bryncrug, with a husband

and children of her own, and the care of
a home for which she alone was responsible;
with new duties, and fresh cares, Mary's love
for her Bible had grown, not diminished.

Other things had changed—companion-
ships, home influences, claims, interests—but
the Sacred Word remained to her unaltered,
except that every day it grew more into her
heart, and became more one with her life,
yielding her, in answer to careful study, and
earnest prayer for God's Spirit of enlightenment, deep meanings of truth and sweetness
which had hitherto been unperceived.

If Mary's life was a busy one during the
years spent at Llanfihangel, doubly so was
her life here at Bryncrug. But the same
quiet energy and steadfastness of purpose for
which she had ever been remarkable still
pervaded all that she did, making every
duty, however humble and homely, a service
for Christ, while by her consistent Christian
walk and example she influenced for good
all that were about her.

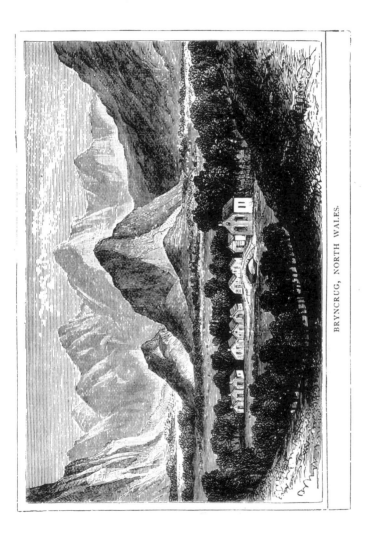

BRYNCRUG, NORTH WALES.

If a neighbour's child wished to have a Sunday-school lesson explained, she invariably came to Mary, who could always spare a few minutes to give the instruction that had been so precious to her in her youthful days. And her intimate knowledge of the Bible gave her a very clear way of explaining its truths, while her insight into character, and her sympathetic nature, made her a wise counsellor and an acceptable teacher.

If, again, a friend wanted a hint or two in the making of a new dress, or advice as to the management of her bee-hives, Mary was always the authority appealed to, as being the most capable, as well as the kindest of neighbours, and ever ready to lend a helping hand, or speak a helpful word.

Thus in Bryncrug she was winning for herself the love and confidence of her fellow-creatures, and showing forth in life and character the glory of that Saviour whose faithful handmaid she tried to be.

We have just alluded to the fact of her

being an authority in the management of bees, and she was justly considered so, as her success with her own bee-hives sufficiently proved.

That success was simply remarkable, both as to the large number of hives, and their profitable results.

The attracting power and influence which Mary seemed to exercise over people appeared to extend even to her bees; but, be this as it might, we are told that whenever she approached the hives, her reception by her winged subjects was nothing less than royal, such was the loyalty and enthusiasm of these sensible, busy little honey-makers.

The air would be thick with buzzing swarms, and presently they would alight upon her by hundreds, covering her from head to foot, walking over her, but never attempting to sting, or showing any feeling but one of absolute confidence and friendliness. She would even catch a handful of them as though they had been so many flies—but softly, so as not to hurt them—and they never misunderstood her, or offered her the slightest injury. In short, there seemed to be a sort of tacit agreement between Mary and her bees, and they were apparently proud and pleased that a part of what they were the means of earning should go towards the support of God's work in the world. For Mary divided the proceeds thus :

The money brought by the sale of the honey was used for the family and household expenses, but the proceeds of the wax were divided among the societies which, poor as she was, Mary delighted to assist.

Among these, foremost in her estimation stood the British and Foreign Bible Society, with the establishment of which she had been so closely connected, and she was never happier than when she could spare what for her was a large sum, to help in sending the Word of God—so precious to her own heart—over the world.

Mary was also much interested in the

Calvinistic Methodist Missionary Society—
a Society founded by the denomination to
which she had, for so many years, belonged ;
and many a secret self-denial could have borne
witness to her generosity in giving of her
substance for the furtherance of the Gospel.

On one occasion we are told that, when
a collection was made at Bryncrug for the
China Million Testament Fund, in the year
1854, a ten-shilling gold piece was found
in the collection plate, neatly wrapped up
between half-pence, and thus hidden until
the money came to be counted.

This was Mary's gift, the outcome of a
loving, generous heart touched by God's
love and the spiritual wants of her fellow-
creatures.

Mary was sitting at her cottage door one
day, when a neighbour, Betsy Davies, came
up. "Good day, Mary," said she ; "may I
come and sit with you for an hour this
afternoon ? I've a dress I must alter for my
eldest girl, and I don't see how to begin, so

I thought may be you'd be good enough to show me."

"Yes, that I will, with pleasure," replied Mary. "My children are all at school, and my husband has gone to Towyn, so I have a quiet hour or two before me. Let me see your work, Betsy."

Betsy Davies laid the garment over Mary's knee, and Mary's eyes, quick and intelligent as ever, saw in a moment or two what was needed.

"That's not a difficult job," said she pleasantly, "nor yet a long one. Just unpick that seam, Betsy, and I'll pin it for you as it ought to be; then if you let down the tuck in the skirt, you'll have it long enough, and as for the rent in the stuff, I think I've got some thread about the right colour with which you can darn it up. I will show you, my dear, how I darn my little Mary's dresses when she tears them, as she does very often, playing with her brothers. Yours can be mended just in the same way, and you'll see the place will hardly show at all."

When the two women had settled down to their work, Betsy said, " I wish you'd tell me, Mary, how you manage to get on as you do. You can't be rich people, your husband being only a weaver like mine and like most of the others here, and yet you never get into debt, and you always seem to have enough for yourselves, and what's more wonderful still, you've enough to give away something too ; I must say I can't understand it ! "

" I don't think there's anything very hard to understand," said Mary, smiling. " If by great care and a little self-denial we can contribute something of our substance to help on God's work, it is surely the greatest joy we can have."

" Yes, that's all very well," replied Betsy, " but I never have anything to contribute ; and yet I haven't as many children as you, and so my family and housekeeping doesn't cost so much."

" It's like this, Betsy dear," said Mary,
"we ask ourselves—I mean my husband, and
my children, and I, all of us—'What can
we do without ? ' And one and another is
willing to give up some little indulgence, and
so we save the money. This we put into
a box which we call the treasury, and whenever we add anything to what we keep there,
we think of the widow who cast into the
treasury of the temple her two mites, and of
our Lord's kind, tender words about her."

" But what sort of things can you give
up ? " asked Betsy.   " We   poor folk, it
seems to me, don't have any more than just
the necessaries of life, and one can't give up
eating and drinking, or go without clothes to
our backs."

"Yet I think if you consider a bit, you'll
see there are some trifles which are not really
needful, though they may be pleasant," replied
Mary.   " Now for instance, Thomas had
always been used to a pipe and a bit of
tobacco in an evening after his work was

done ; but when we were all wondering what we could give up for our dear Lord's sake he said, 'Well, wife, I'll give up my smoke in the evenings.' And I tell you, Betsy, the tears came into my eyes when I heard that, knowing that my husband's words meant a real sacrifice. Then our eldest son, wishing to imitate his father, cried out, 'And I've still got that Christmas box my master gave me last winter, and I'll give that.' And Sally, she gave up the thought of a new hat ribbon I'd promised her, and she sponged and ironed her old one instead, and wore it, feeling prouder than if it had been new. And as for little Benny, he was all one day picking up sticks in the wood to earn a penny, and that was his gift."

"And you yourself?" asked Betsy, with interest.

"I? Oh, I have the wax that my bees make ; and the money that I got by selling that went into the treasury, as well as any other small sum I did not actually need.

And this I must say, Betsy, we have never really suffered for the want of anything we have given to God; and He repays us with such happiness and content as He alone can give."

"That I can well believe," rejoined Betsy, "for I never hear you grumble, or see you look cross or discontented like the rest of the neighbours, and as I do myself only too often. Well, Mary," she continued, "I mean to try your plan, though it will come very hard at first, as I'm not used to that sort of saving."

"I think I got used to it when I was a child, putting away my little mites of money towards buying a Bible," rejoined Mary, "For six years I put by all my little earnings, and since then it has come natural."

"You did get your Bible, then?"

"Yes, indeed; this is the very one," and rising from her seat Mary took the much prized volume from the little table in the cottage, and put it into her visitor's hands.

Betsy looked at it, inside and out, then handed it back saying, " I really believe, Mary, that this Bible is one of the reasons why you are so different from all the rest of us. You've read and studied and learnt so much of it, that your thoughts and words and life are full of it."

And Mary turned her bright dark eyes, now full of happy tears, upon her companion, and answered in a broken voice—

" O Betsy dear, if there is a little, even a little truth in what you kindly say of me, I thank God that in His great mercy and love He suffers me, poor and weak and simple as I am, to show forth in my small way His glory, and the truth of His blessed Word."

Nunquam Frustra.   " *Never in Vain.*"

(*From a Bible in the Society's Library.*)

RUINS OF MARY JONES'S COTTAGE.

CHAPTER X.

HER WORKS DO FOLLOW HER.

O mighty tree, o'ershadowing all the earth,
In loneliest wilds thy seedling had its birth.

NOW our narrative nears its close. The last glimpse of our friend Mary shows us an aged woman clad in the curious old Welsh dress.

She holds in one hand a staff for the support of her trembling limbs, once so

MARY JONES IN HER LATER YEARS.

active and nimble ; while with the other she clasps to her side her beloved Bible, the companion of so many years, the consoler and comforter, the guide and teacher of her life.

How much of joy or of sorrow, of trial or of what the world calls success, had fallen to Mary's lot during her long life of eighty-two years, we know not. We learn that she had eight children, several of whom may have died in early life. One son, we believe, is living now [1882], having made his home in America.

Little as we know, however, of Mary's actual experiences, it was impossible that during her married life she should not have learned what deep sorrow meant, as it is almost certain that she survived several of her children, and quite certain that her husband too died before she did.

Still, since we are taught that God's children do not sorrow as those without hope, so we are sure that the childlike, trusting spirit of this handmaid of the Lord was as ready to suffer as to do the will of the Divine Master, and that however deep the affliction, there was no bitterness in the grief, no despair in the tears that watered the graves of loved ones gone before.

Feeble and tottering was now our once bright, bonny, blithe maiden, but it was only physically that Mary was altered. She was still the same brave, simple-hearted, earnest, faithful follower of Christ. Time with its changes, in parting her from most of those whom she loved on earth, had not separated her from the love of Jesus, or taken away her delight in the Word of the Lord that endureth for ever.

Indeed she loved her Bible better even than of old, for she understood it more fully, and had proved its truth beyond all doubting, again and again, in her daily life for so many years.

Can we doubt, then, that when the summons came, and she heard the voice which she had known and loved from childhood, saying to her " Come up higher !" she had no fears, no shrinking, but felt that surely since goodness and mercy had followed her all the days of her life, she should dwell in the house of the Lord—that house above, not made with hands—for ever.

Mary Jones died December the 28th, 1866, at the good old age of eighty-two. We have no particulars of her last moments, save that on her death-bed she bequeathed her precious Bible to the Rev. Robert Griffiths, who in his turn bequeathed it to Mr. Rees.

This Bible, which is now in the possession of the British and Foreign Bible Society, is a thick octavo, of the edition published by the Society for the Promotion of Christian Knowledge, in 1799—the last edition of the Welsh Bible previous to the establishment of the Bible Society.

The volume contains, in addition to the actual text of the now recognized and authorized Scripture, John Cannes' marginal

references, the Apocrypha, the Book of
Common Prayer, a metrical version of the
Psalms by Edmund Prys, and various Church
tables. It also contains, in Mary Jones's
handwriting — in perhaps the first English

that she had learned — a note that she
bought it in the year 1800, when she was
sixteen years old.

So full of days, and like Dorcas of old,

of good works, Mary Jones passed away from earth to the rest that remaineth for the people of God ; a sheaf of ripe corn safely garnered at last in the heavenly granary.

She was buried in the little churchyard at Bryncrug, and a stone has been raised to her memory by those who loved to recall the influence of her beautiful life, and the important if humble part she had taken in the founding of the great work of the British and Foreign Bible Society.

FAC-SIMILE OF WRITING ON THE BIBLE

GRAVE OF MARY JONES.

(Probably the age should be given as 80, since Mary Jones appears to have been born in 1784.

A GUIDE TO THE MARY JONES COUNTRY.

THE cottage where Mary Jones lived as a child is situated at Tyn-y-fach (National Grid 673 095) in the parish of Llanfihangel-y-pennant, about two miles from Abergynolwyn. Tywyn, the nearest town, is on the coast, about six miles west of Abergynolwyn.

Approaching from Welshpool by the A 470 road the left-hand turn should be taken at the Cross Foxes Hotel and joining there the A 487, the range of mountains known as Cader Idris, over which Mary walked barefooted to Bala, can be seen stretching some seven miles on the right-hand side.

After four miles the B 4405 leaves to the right at Minffordd and, skirting Tal-y-llyn Lake, enters Abergynolwyn. In the centre of the village, the road leading off to the right is taken and, passing the Post Office, it soon climbs bearing to the left at the end

of the village. After about a mile, the right-
hand road should be followed; this leads
into a lane, passing the parish church and
at the extreme end, close to the bridge over
the River Afon, is the ruined cottage and
memorial to Mary Jones.

Mary Jones is buried at Bryncrug (610
033) in the graveyard behind the chapel.
The village is about four miles west of
Abergynolwyn and if the right-hand turn is
taken where the B 4405 joins the A 493 and
another right-hand turn made immediately
over the river bridge, the large chapel will
be seen to the right.

Retracing the route through Bryncrug
back to the A 493 but, instead of turning
back over the bridge, proceeding a few
yards northwards toward Dolgellau, Mary
Jones spent her closing years in the last
house in the village on the left-hand side
(607 034).

Thomas Charles (1755–1814) is still honoured in Bala, plaques on the wall of

Barclays Bank in the main street recording the house in which he resided. His statue is outside a chapel in a road leading off the main street on the same side as the Bank.

It has not proved possible to trace the school and chapel at Abergynolwyn which Mary attended but it is believed to be now used as three cottages at the foot of the hill leading into the village at a place known as Curt.

Thousands have been touched by the story of how
a poor Welsh girl walked barefooted to Bala
(twenty-five miles from her home) to buy a Bible
for which she had been saving for several years.
This is the original telling of the Mary Jones
story, which for years was out of print, and
includes the Victorian illustrations.

GOSPEL STANDARD TRUST PUBLICATIONS
12(b) Roundwood Lane, Harpenden, Herts AL5 3DD, E...

ISBN 0-903556-69-3